T0062998

Knowledge for the Next Time

How to Use Monday's Trials to Relieve Tuesday's Tribulations

KAJLI PRINCE

abbott press

Abbott Press books may be ordered through booksellers or by contacting:

Abbott Press
1663 Liberty Drive
Bloomington, IN 47403
www.abbottpress.com
Phone: 1 (866) 697-5310

ISBN: 978-1-4582-1898-8 (sc)
ISBN: 978-1-4582-1899-5 (e)

Library of Congress Control Number: 2015908415

Print information available on the last page.

Abbott Press rev. date: 07/06/2015

CONTENTS

DEDICATION

This book is the product of my personal experiences, those with family, and with friends past and present. However, most of the experiences I contemplate here extend from activities with the two most special women in my life: my wife, Ronla, and my daughter, Kahlia. Their love and support allow me to bend light with my mind. Yes, their wonderfulness gives me superpowers.

Cheers!

PREFACE

When you look back on your life experiences, how many critical stages do you feel you were unprepared for: dating, finances, children, work, family, and aging?

I am now in my forties, forty-two years young to be exact. I have been through my fair share of life's ups and downs … and ups and downs (repeat). My disposition toward life's challenges has been seasoned with a bit of philosophy, some cynicism, and a healthy punch of LMAO. Some might say it's a uniquely broad perspective. I've had some legal education as well as teaching experience. I'm also a pretty damn good cook.

What inspired me to write this book is the never-ending question of *how to do better*. How do I more effectively use my day-to-day experiences to help nurture a healthy level of growth and development? I've always had a dedication to improvement, but I have a family now and after five years of marriage and three years of fatherhood I can see how much more critical it is to have that *balance* and *resilience* necessary to be successful in any important endeavor. To be able to build the skills necessary to navigate circumstances more effectively and efficiently.

Change—not just mediocre change but substantive, effective change—is tough to generate. However, change is critical to improvement because it is that *change in choice in the moment* that produces a different outcome. Hindsight would be great if it came before the task. But to successfully complete the task to our own "true" satisfaction, we often need to change our "typical" actions in the moment. Hindsight often leads us to say, "If I could only go back and do it again, knowing what I know now …"

Knowledge for the Next Time begins a journey that touches on this very real feeling and shows how to glean more useful take-aways from our life experiences, for the next time. This can be going back to our teens and doing it better, coming back as a hamster and revolutionizing hamster living, or, more practically, using Monday's trials to relieve Tuesday's tribulations.

INTRODUCTION

I believe people are generally good natured. Our families are usually what motivate us most. Children especially drive us to reach for more. Your children push you to eat vegetables you may well have never eaten if not for attempting to model good habits for their benefit. You might find yourself driven to be more outgoing, with trips to the park, the library, or camping. Your time with them allows you to get more exercise.

However, as any parent can attest, kids drive you nuts! I have a three-year-old, and I often find myself just staring blankly at nothing trying to figure out what the hell is going on around me. *How am I going to get through the next twelve and one-half seconds of this minute?* I wonder. *How am I going to get out of the house this morning to take her to daycare?* Getting out of the house, especially in the morning, often feels like *Escape from Alcatraz*—such contrasting emotions of fear and relief. How did our parents do it?

Family as a whole presents us with much the same contradiction. We love them, but they often have the potential to most easily drive us crazy. We can deal with strangers because they don't know any better. But family and those close to us really know us, so we can get a little scratchy when they do something that irks us. This potential for tension is always there, and so interaction and contact with others can exhaust us. But interaction is the most critical part of a relationship. Otherwise there is no real connection. But with all the possible volatility, how does it all work successfully?

The glue that brings it all together is us—that is, you, the individual. Your temperament, perception, discipline, and balance as an individual directly affects your broader interactions. Therefore, working on yourself as a person is working on your relationships. Your disposition is critical to the affiliation. As such, learning how to nurture your personality is essential, not just to your individual success but also to the success of your community, especially your family. Are you disciplined enough, however, to sow the seeds of change?

THE MISSION

How can I do better? The answer, I decided, is that I need to develop myself using my experiences while developing my experiences to further my development. That is, the best plan of action for effecting change is by making better choices and reflecting on past choices. This self-development will lead not just to individual success but also family success. After all, our first real focus as adults is our immediate families. For me, it's my wife and my baby girl.

With this I am ready for the next challenge. What follows is my own attempts to analyze my past experiences and to mine out the lessons I can apply toward the future, as well as some tips for you along the way. This is an analysis that folds into itself; that is, the optimization process is happening with each evaluation, leading up to the point at which I am ready for the next challenge. These are just the first lines on the blueprint. Awareness is just the beginning.

CHAPTER 1

Potty Training

I have a daughter, my one and only child. She is my *joy and pride*. She turned three years old this past year, and I am finally starting to see the resemblance she has to me. Kahlia—her name is a combination of my wife's name, Ronla, and my name, Kajli. The "h" in her name is reflective of the misspelling of my name when I was born. As the story goes, my name was supposed to be spelled Kahli. So the combination would then be the original spelling of my name and the last letter of my wife's name: Kahlia.

What a wonderful little girl. Of course, I'm biased, but that doesn't change the fact that she beams with an energy that anyone can see right away. She is very independent. Her ability to focus lends to an impressive attention to detail. Physically she's built like a soccer player or Olympic-level gymnast.

But—I refer to her sometimes as "Chiren," my shorthand, almost southern way of saying "children." What I mean is she is more than just one child. She is more like a plurality of children all rolled up into one. She is like eight handfuls.

Her personality covers the trinity, and there is some extra source of energy in there that pushes her even further. Having said that, I still describe her as keeping whoever is caring for her "constructively" busy. But it is exhausting.

I am a teacher at heart. In the past I have taught all ages of students. So it gives me a different kind of pleasure to see how well my daughter is developing. And the objective feedback we get is just as positive. For her three-year pediatric visit, the doctor was thrilled with her. She was attentive and interacted with her environment and the people in it; she knew her name, sex, and age; and she even listened to and obeyed me while we were there.

All this I see in her highlights an appreciation for my comprehensive effort to interact with her on a consistent basis and to expose her to different activities, including fishing, arts and crafts, construction, biking, play gyms, museums, and cooking. But, again, it's exhausting. She has single-handedly stretched her daddy in ways he didn't know he could stretch.

Potty training embodies the next level of teaching for me. Since it's my own child, it's obviously a more intimate lesson than those from all of my years of teaching. However, potty training does have some very fundamental elements of teaching (in any situation): patience, patience, patience; active engagement (with respect to encouragement and positive feedback); consistency; and even more patience. Everyone has a different temperament. So what might seem straight forward for one may well be a struggle for another. For me, as equipped as I felt I was for kids, actually being a parent pushed me a lot farther than I thought I would have to go, naturally. You can't know the all-encompassing "thing" being a parent is until you become one.

THE BREAKDOWN

At the end of the day the objective is to use my many experiences and core proficiencies to be a better person, husband, and father. This analysis can also be characterized as a discussion; a collection of random conversations with people about family, hard work, and discipline; and a recollection of relevant thoughts regarding the same.

And of course, given my true passion, this is an in-depth philosophical deliberation of human dynamics and self-actualization.

PART I

Threes

I'm doing well with my objective, moving forward through it all, aging gracefully like a fine wine. But what of a little context? Some appreciation of where I came from would put whatever progress I have made into a little more perspective. Moreover, a working knowledge of my past and present personality would also better highlight how I have used my new self-development method to change my reality—evidence that this method is not just words on a page but a guiding principle bearing fruit. With that said, let me have some fun describing myself using a food analogy.

Three is a favorite number of mine. There is a lot of divinity in the number three. For my purposes, I will elaborate on three basic characteristics that define me as an individual. These three characteristics are also arguably the three most important flavor profiles to balance when cooking—especially for savory dishes: sweet, spicy, and salty.

CHAPTER 2

Sweet

I wanna have my cake, eat it, and not get fat!

Let the good I have done and continue to do crush the foolish and borderline criminal acts I still find necessary to commit. And why not pay me a ton of money for simply wanting to do a good job? Isn't it the thought that counts? Oh, and if I must work, why don't I work the weekends and have the weekdays off? I'll have the same number of holidays, but all I require moving forward is a two-day work week.

It'll never happen. You may think only a lazy person would ask for those things. However, it also likely resonates (at least a bit) because we all have routines that leave us drained. "I'm overworked and underpaid," he cried.

It's the theme of many books and movies: the guy in the office who has six different bosses constantly pressing him for the same report or the stewardess constantly dealing with pissed-off and unruly passengers. When these regular folk snap and "break ranks," they become heroes to many because we can feel their pain.

Do I feel like my feet are held to the fire for all my missteps? No. But I'm still waiting for the bag of money to fall from the sky into my living room, right at my feet. The bag, of course, contains enough tax-free cash to pay off all my bills (including my student loans), with enough left over to live like a rock star … or at least a pebble star.

TITHES AND OFFERINGS

My spiritual life is storied. I was born. At some point I became Catholic. As a child I was exposed to other Christian denominations, including Baptist, Lutheran, and Episcopalian, but never Seventh Day Adventist—the denomination I currently identify with. While I am an SDA Christian, I still have space in my brain for science, for theories like evolution and the Big Bang. I was exposed to science as much as, if not more than, I was exposed to Christianity.

Still, I believe in my heart that belief in God (regardless of the God you believe in) is necessary for a full life. To me God represents sacrifices. If your God doesn't look like or sound like my God, my sacrifice is to accept that. I still need to respect you and be able to interact with you with genuineness.

In that regard, I try to follow Jesus's example. I haven't finished reading all the stories in the Bible yet, but I get the sense that Jesus was a bit unbiased when it came to people. Prostitute? No problem. Murderer? Hey, you're cool with me. Thief? Well, maybe you needed that item more than I did. The point is we all deserve the same love and respect.

Like most, I am a work in progress. I wish my perceived struggles counted as tithes and my givebacks as offerings. If so, I believe I would be in good standing with the Church.

My former pastor spoke often about the Church's involvement in community activities, talking to people outside the Church about God, and the good things he has done for others. Part of this call to arms was a warning. His plea was directed at those parishioners who didn't have any extenuating responsibilities beyond themselves—that is, those who were not responsible for children or elderly family members.

His call to action made me think, even long after that sermon. I wondered if God would count my life struggles as consideration for my back tithes. I wondered if my work as a teacher (and by default a mentor, councilor, and confidant) served as offerings, in addition to those I have given to the Church over the years. I realized these hopes might be wishful thinking. Everyone has life struggles to deal with, excuses not to give back to others, yet we are still called to tithe and give offerings whenever possible.

The point is if I have these thoughts, I'm probably not the only one. So perhaps next time a pastor makes this plea, I should put it out there and start a conversation.

I think if I had been more steeped in spirituality at a younger age, I would be in a different place right now. But for now, I'll keep moving in the direction I'm moving in. The truth is that I try to be good and do good for the Church, but I am a father and a teacher. I'm a busy man. But maybe next time I will have more resources in place and more time to do more in the present. It is a work in progress.

FOOD

Yes, please!

I love food that fits in my mouth … even if I have to give it a little nudge or a good shove. But these days it's impossible not to be ever-aware that food makes us fat. I start eating some chips, and it's like, "Oh yeah. That's what I'm talking about." Then I see the nutrition facts on the back of the bag: 120 calories—okay; 59 grams of fat—not bad; serving size, 1 chip; servings per container, 100 chips—*what?!* I did math in school. Yep, that one bag of yummy chips has now fattened you another 12,000 calories. Of course, this is an exaggeration, but the point is I can no longer guiltlessly enjoy a whole bag of chips.

Food can be such a drug. Even athletes find themselves unable to change their eating habits once they've stopped playing and then often end up putting on a lot of weight, since they are not burning calories like they used to. All that to say—food is not just a "fat" person problem.

So how can my past experiences with food better my future? Well, next time I should try to change the way I look at food. At this point I know most of the dos and don'ts, so it's not a matter of ignorance. Rather, I need to be more aware of the pitfalls. And there are lots of pitfalls: eating while watching TV; eating late at night; indulging when I feel like a sandwich, a burger, or an ice cream sundae. Next time I want to gorge on chips, I'll think about the consequences, think about my long-term happiness rather than the fulfilling of an immediate craving. Next time I want a sandwich (the sandwich: two pieces of bread, meat, cheese, and mayo), maybe I'll make one with no mayo, with less bread, and with some lettuce.

Ugh. I shudder at the thought.

CHAPTER 3

Spicy

Why don't I look like the sexy, savvy bitch I feel like?

I like it hot. And yes, I'm talking about sex. I'm talking about food, trouble, you name it. My inner me says, "Take it to the limit!" I'd describe myself as impulsive.

I still like to put my hand in "D butta," if you know what I mean. But I've had to grow up, to get my grown-man savvy on. I'm a family man now. Therefore, no more sex in public, while driving, or with different women. I've had to settle down. Easier said than done.

That's not exactly what it might sound like. The tough part, I find, is getting comfortable with such a different pace. Consider, again, potty training. Now a new person needs regular access to the bathroom, in addition to my wife. It's not just me anymore.

Sometimes I think about how much easier it was to sit on my throne before I had a family. Not to mention that sexy nights with the wife are a bit fewer and farther between than before the potty training.

BEFORE THE RING AND THE RATTLE

This is where I get to floss a bit, where I talk about how I used to get my mack on. Mind you, I was always a little bourgeois. Growing up, my family had a little change, so we had a pretty good lifestyle. We traveled, went out to eat, went to good schools, and as kids we had one of the first personal computers.

But that's not what I'm talking about. As an adult, I ramped up my lifestyle a good bit when I started working and making my own coin, most notably when I was working on Wall Street. The Street was like ground zero for men with too much money and not enough morals. It was fun while it lasted and certainly appealed to the ladies.

Wall Street movies, like *The Wolf of Wall Street*, are actually pretty good depictions of the debauchery that goes on there. Although my experience wasn't nearly that dramatic. After about a year and a half of climbing the ladder at Spear, Leeds and Kellogg (eventually acquired by Goldman Sachs), I had my own office with a window.

Unlike the movies, my extravagances were more like car service to and from work and bonuses throughout the year when the company did well. I remember I got my first bonus after just two months with the company. We received Tens of thousands of dollars in end-of-year bonuses. I had dry-cleaning service to the office, manicures at least twice a week—with clear nail polish to add that regal thing, and tailored suits from Paris. There was a shop across the street from the office that had the best fabrics on the street. This was around the millennium, and we all had two-way pagers. So I could spend a couple hours in that shop picking out the coldest suit patterns and still be talking to clients on my pager like I was at my desk.

What's crazy is those were only the times when I was spending my own money. The managing directors and the partners would take their people out to eat, drink, and raid gentlemen's lounges up and down Manhattan. I felt like a kid in a candy shop. It was disgusting, and yet beautiful at the same time.

But it wasn't a long-term career. The unspoken word on the street was, "If you don't reach management in four to five years, find another gig." This was before the financial crisis, and unless your eyes were wide shut, you knew it was coming. So I left the candy shop and pursued a career in intellectual property law. This took me to law school in Michigan and then ultimately to Northern Virginia and the Department of Commerce.

CHAPTER 4

Salty

At this point, can I just get out at least half of what I put in?

Some folks are straight conspiracy theorists: "The government has been spying on me ever since I figured out that the president is a communist jihadi implant." Others are more optimistic: "The police are my friends." I, on the other hand, would be somewhere between those two positions.

For example, a certain comedian responded to a widely debated perception that black people have better lives today, than during, say, the days of slavery or even the days of the civil rights movement. He suggested that we should never have been hung from trees and swing sets in the first place. His point was, how can our lives be considered "better" when the comparable premise is often based on very disturbing and inhumane circumstances? His point made sense to me, and I will set my level of cynicism there for now.

Of course, apathy is not beyond me either. The world is going to hell in a handbasket. Well, not quite. The world, and its handbasket, is a lot smaller these days. The Internet, social media, and Oprah provide so much more information than was readily available just a decade ago. Arguably for the better, technology connects and informs us. For the worse, we are exposed to tons more vile, disgusting trash than before. But that's hardly determinative of a world gone bad. Just think how much cruddier things look in your bedroom under a black light or how your *"belly gut"* profile looks in the mirror before you vacuum seal yourself into your spanks. The trash was always there; we just didn't see it before.

BOYS IN THE HOOD

Growing up, I saw a lot. And based on some perspective I've gained as an adult, I do think the world has changed for the better (if barely). For example, working on Wall Street made me realize that there was no All-Powerful Man who woke up in the morning to hold minorities back. Listen, the guys at the top didn't care if your race was blue mixed with indigo. As long as you were dependable, knew the products, and could move them or could fix their trading system when it went down—in short, as long as you could do your job—you were good with them.

NO FREEBIES

Still, the glass ceiling is real in my experience, but it's a lot higher up than I was led to believe growing up. Over my career I've done good work as well as bad, and I've usually gotten feedback accordingly. When I realized this, I shifted to a mentality of "Stop dragging your ass and get proficient." I suppose this idea skips over some underlying socioeconomic obstacles, but I do believe that success is still out there for the taking. Of course, to get it, you first you have to stop and work on yourself.

WAIT ... WHAT?

It would be nice to succeed at everything, for all my work to pay off, and to always be in good favor. I wouldn't have any problems because I could easily fix anything that came up. Wouldn't that be cool?

But how practical is that? When we embrace the fact that we have to fail to succeed, we become that much stronger. To say I "have" to fail is not to say that the only way I can do well is to go through pain and suffering as a result of falling short of my goals. This just means that the more I aspire to, the more hurdles I will encounter. The walk to my goals will undoubtedly present unknown challenges. So unless I am supremely lucky, I am going to fall down every now and then, no matter my best efforts.

Failure is inevitable. However, a healthy balance of success and failure should ultimately lead to overall achievement.

PAIN

Pain has no target, no bias. It doesn't care about your skin color, financial status, weight, or sexual preference. It comes from the unknown to your awareness, from tough losses to unexpected gains, and from nowhere and everywhere. Any circumstance you find yourself in, pain can rear its ugly head.

I had a boss who once told me you have to have a thick skin to succeed. That notion always stuck with me, probably because I found it to be true. Toughness is one of those characteristics you can't just want to have. Toughness is something that is tested. It's difficult to be tough in the face of pain at first, and you never quite get it right. But you just have to keep drawing from those experiences, and your resilience will gradually build.

WHERE *"TOOK"* MY SPIRIT?

As adults, life has a way of weighing us down. Toughness may be a necessary advantage, but it can grow tiresome. And despite the bounties in my life, at some point I sensed that I had lost my vitality. It became obvious to me that I was more so existing than living.

I didn't know why, but I eventually realized I was going to have to dig down into my soul to find out.

What makes my pulse pulsate? I found my vitality in that question. It was dehydrated, discolored, and decrepit, but I found it. When had I lost it? How long had it been since I had energy that was pure—not recycled from anger, or hatred, or shame, but raw energy, energy born from a healthy spirit?

So what to make of a life so far lived? By all accounts I had it all but still felt hollowed out. What do I do with that in the future?

Life is full of tests, and this road I am on is there to get me where I have asked to go. Like Job, all kings are tested. The crucible scorches, but it doesn't burn; it sharpens. It changes the color and texture of your resolve.

I must remember that future challenges are not just meaningless obstacles but simply new turns on my path. Challenges bring lessons, which bring perspective. Looking back, my life makes more sense now. The present is a divine vantage point, a reward for persistent patience.

PART II

The Fourth Dimension

.

Now you have a little more perspective on *"the me that is me."* If you can relate to part I, then this project was worth the effort. If you're worried about your own sanity, that's okay; you're cool with me. Misery loves company.

Part II introduces a new dynamic: time, the fourth dimension. I realize that sounds like something out of a sci-fi movie. It kind of is, but not quite. Time takes us a step beyond the theme of three that I used to describe my personality. Just bear with me for a tick.

Two points makes a line, but three points makes a plane. So picture yourself standing in your living room. You are a three-dimensional figure standing right there in the middle of the room. Now add time. You are standing in your living room at 4 p.m. on Tuesday, March 3, when a bag of money falls from the sky and lands at your feet—tax free. Wonderful. Best day of your life.

Now let's pick a different time. You're still standing in your living room, but it's a Friday in November. It's Dooms Day. Rage and pestilence burst through the roof of your living room and carry you down to hell in the world's hand basket.

Two different scenarios, same living room. Okay, enough science fiction.

The point is you can literally be standing in the same spot and, depending on *time*, experience two different realities. The relevance of this to our greater discussion is our perception of ourselves. This gets into something I call *the Delta*, but I will elaborate on that a little more later.

For now, I refer to time in relation to the act of freeing ourselves from the incongruity of thinking we are that which we are not—or at least not yet—as well as how liberating it can be when we carefully change that paradigm. But let's take a look at some basic precepts and traditions that foster this phenomenon.

THE TIME PROBLEM

It's difficult to use the time we are given wisely.

We tend to rush through time, especially when things are difficult or stressful. During those tough times our vision gets clouded, largely due to the expectations (of others and ourselves) to succeed. It's like taking a timed test. During it, you struggle to remember the right answers. I've taken my fair share, and I've noticed that as soon as the test is over, I then suddenly have all the answers. Once there are no more expectations, I can see clearly. In this way, it's these tough times that change us because after they're over, we see with more clarity.

CHOICE AND CHANGE

Often we are driven by speculation of how an experience will play out and how it will affect us, as opposed to just waiting to see how it goes. We project an outcome. However, projection is the opposite of change because it robs you of your choice to do things differently.

Think of how you might react if someone came up to you and told you the outcome for a given situation. Going back to the exam analogy, what if a classmate told you before the exam that you were going to fail? This probably isn't true, but that person's comment would psych you out. You might be hell bent on clearing your head and doing the best you could to conquer the exam (so you could go back and tell that *hater* to shove it), but you're more likely to choke than you were before his comment.

Time is a tricky concept to master. So how *does* one tackle time?

CHAPTER 5

The Past

I am used to hard work, or what I consider hard work anyway. My dad has had a roofing and waterproofing business ever since I was a small child, so naturally I felt like I grew up on a roof. Heck, I might have been conceived up there. What I knew pretty early on, however, was that I had no desire to inherit the family business.

Here's the thing about roofs: They're wicked hot. You often have to climb up more than a few flights of stairs to get to them. Other times a shaky ladder paves the way. I grew up in the age of the personal computer. I was more interested in an air-conditioned cubicle than a precarious, sunbaked rooftop.

THE PAYCHECK

I find work tough, really tough, especially when a lot of my livelihood is wrapped up in it. There always seem to be hurdles, and no matter what kind of career you have, there are always highs and lows. Sometimes you don't get out what you've put in. But then, you will never get out what you haven't put in either.

Here's my feel-good commentary on work: It sucks, but it defines and sustains us. It hones us, our personalities and skills, as much as, if not more than, anything else. There is great motivation in it, but it does tend to consume us. It leaves us with limited time for hobbies and loved ones. We miss the growth and development of our children, leaving it to nannies and teachers to make those precious connections. A grandparent might well find they are desperate to have a close relationship with their grandchildren because they already missed their chance with their own children.

The work-life balance—it's a tough dynamic.

WORK FOR LIFE

Somehow it dawned on me years ago that if I was going to allow work to consume me, I should at least cultivate a career with a huge quality-of-life component. But that was just one critical component. It would also have to force me to work on myself, on my idiosyncrasies and my weaknesses. Work would have to change me. Ultimately, work would have to balance me out. That way, I would essentially be paid to nurture my own growth—to do better. In that way, work would allow me to be the best me.

So how did I do this? My method was simple: Rather than the "fake it till you make it" approach to work, I treated my tasks with more of an *authentic pursuit* of critical proficiencies in an increasingly more reasonable timeframe. In this way, I was able to learn more and take more ownership over better-quality projects and, thus, take real pride in what I was doing.

CHAPTER 6

The Present

On the road of life, we are constantly changing lanes, trying to find the best approach to our end destination, juggling different priorities. Nowadays I try to find a good lane and just stay in it. This is much simpler to do when you only have one task. Figure out what you need to do, position yourself so that you can accomplish the goal, and keep working on it. However, the more responsibilities you add to that model, the more difficult it is to position yourself. Even with just three goals—self, family, and work—something seems destined to suffer, even if just a little.

But you stick with it, like that tough workout with the new personal trainer, working new muscles of balance and discipline (all the while trying not to pass out). It's not easy. *Sure, I'm in shape, but my shape is round … or pear-shaped. I can't just keep jumping and kicking and lifting and moving constantly like that,* I think. But I have to keep working until my body gets used to it.

Our balance and discipline muscles now toned, we can get through any challenge. But it's not enough to just get through; we have to reflect on the entire process, soup to nuts, once it's over. We have to learn from that experience and apply that same process to as many other things in our lives as possible. It's all about *knowledge for the next time.*

Don't just go through an experience, come through it, and leave it there, only to go through a similar experience later as if it's the first time. Our experiences are all related. Wealth is not amassed by continually reinventing the wheel, and this philosophy applies to all sorts of aspects of our lives.

LOVE AND RESPECT

I once saw a video by a pastor/doctor about how women feed off of love, while men feed off of respect. When I applied this principle to my own marriage, it seemed to fit. My wife is often offended when I don't do things that reflect a loving sentiment. And times I've gotten irate seem to be related to feeling disrespected.

To me, my wife's "disrespect" can include not appreciating my efforts to support our family, assuming my shortcomings are going to become a way of life, and accusing me of never listening to her.

Luckily, I can use this love/respect principle and our past disagreements toward future ones. Next time I will try to remember to convey a sense of love. Of course, I can't do this effectively without first dealing with my own hang-ups. That is, while I believe not showing love to my wife has mostly to do with her being so hung up on being loved, I'm similarly hung up on being respected. It works both ways, and in this way, we don't realize our respective hang-ups are preventing us from properly interacting with one another.

This concept works more broadly than just in romantic relationships, as well. Consider the different hang-ups we have when dealing with people of other nationalities, religions, and backgrounds. So before you can really communicate with anyone, you have to first deal with the hang-ups getting in your way.

CHAPTER 7

The Future

The future is bright. When you really start to see self-actualization take shape, it's a cool feeling. For one thing, you realize you don't have to be perfect. That's really not what this exercise is about. The key is to be in a position of empowerment, discipline, and calm. The key is to find happiness, even with the imperfections.

When attempting to effect any type of change, you are better suited being confident in your *proven ability*, as opposed to your *expert ability*.

I've discovered I don't need to be an expert; I just need to be confident that I can stick to my plan, my blueprint because that is what is going to take me to the promised land. That is what is going to make me successful. That is what is going to satisfy me and allow me to achieve the goal that I set out for myself.

Objective: Drive to the post office. Result: At the end of the day, I sent my package. Did I take the absolute best route? Am I a perfect, expert driver? No. But I achieved the objective. Next.

THE REARVIEW MIRROR

What's great about memory is that it allows us to look back at our accomplishments. That was something I reminded my students of time and again. The road forward is the road forward: difficult, busy, and exhausting, to say the least. But even a brief look into your rearview mirror should motivate you to keep working hard.

Add to that some basic awareness of your environment, and you should be able to easily see where to position yourself for success. This awareness of what's behind you and around you now should give you the motivation to work toward getting to what's ahead. These are tangible ways we can use time to keep ourselves working at nurturing our better selves.

HONESTY

Be painfully honest with yourself. You don't have to broadcast to the world that you can't set up a conference call, for example, but it helps to know that it isn't your strong suit. Getting caught up in appearances is really just a waste of time. When the need arises, don't volunteer to set up a conference call. If you have to, fake it. If you fail, laugh it off with charm and grace. Remember, you can always ask the tech guy. We all have different skills, and no one's an expert in everything.

It's tough, though not impossible, to be great at something. But if you focus hard enough, you can excel at almost anything. The flip side, though, is that it's totally unnecessary to be great at everything. Think about it. And besides, it's impossible, a wasted effort.

WEALTH

Wealth is comprehensive. Richness is one dimensional. Which would you rather be? For me it's wealth all the way. I don't just mean money, either. It's about being spiritually grounded, mentally sound, physically fit, compassionate, nurturing, light hearted, and intelligent. Forget conference calls. These are the skills we should strive to be great at. This kind of wealth takes on a certain transcendence that is wonderful to experience. Remember, this journey is about a walk to wealth, not a race to rich.

PART III

Elevation

If real change is possible, then that means we are capable of rising above our circumstances. This is another theme that resonates in books and movies. It's the American Dream, a dream that often seems out of touch with reality for so many of us. But it really is achievable; it just depends on what change you aspire to. You want to change your tire? Do it. You want to change your life? You can do that, too.

Now, I realize when one invokes the American Dream, it conjures images of an immigrant coming to America, going to Queens in search of a bride, ready to give up his birthright as a prince back in his African homeland of Zamunda—wait a second … I thought that storyline sounded familiar! But truthfully it makes us think of another immigrant who wants to start her own business here. Notwithstanding what she had to do to get here, after twenty years she has built and maintained a thriving Bodega in *the South of Bronx*. The respect in her story lies in her perseverance, her overcoming of hardships. Maybe one immigrant's efforts paved the way for many more to follow, and on and on.

What are the pillars of that type of personality? How do people take on those types of challenges and produce epic results? How do we elevate ourselves from where we are now? Three characteristics come to mind: balance, discipline, and *choice*.

CHAPTER 8

Balance

*We are our biggest enemies because we are
always with ourselves and notoriously excuse
ourselves for more and more foolishness.*

At the end of the day, self-development comes down to balance. Everything else is prep—the *mise en place* (things in place) to balance's kitchen. Balance is not to be underestimated; it's about having just the *right* amount of something, of many things. Balance includes both extremes, so there are definitely going to be times when we have to sit back and just wait, and times when we are going to have to redline it—keep it 100.

Generally, though, balance is an uneasy quality for us mostly because it pushes us to embrace more change than we are comfortable with. Once when I was in a property law lecture in law school, the professor set up a hypothetical that involved what I would characterize as a little math. When he put his carefully crafted hypothetical to one of the students, she paused a long time, clearly thinking hard. Finally she exclaimed, "I came to law school so I wouldn't have to do math!"

Obviously the incident stuck with me. That was almost ten years ago. I thought it was one of the funniest things I had heard. I taught math for years before that incident, and I thought I had heard all the snarkiest sneers regarding math. People just don't like math, but that is a whole—*nother*—conversation.

The point is I always looked at that woman's inability to do some simple math as an imbalance. Supposedly some people use the right side of their brains, and others use the left side (or some nonsense like that—it never made sense to me). I was a math person, but did that mean I didn't need to be proficient in reading comprehension?

Well as it turns out, I wasn't. It was my stint in law school that really pointed it out once and for all. More specifically, the hard evidence came in the form of an entrance aptitude test. I had suspected for many years that something was off, and the test confirmed it. I did indeed have a reading comprehension deficiency. But at least with that realization, my task became clearer to me.

So how does that relate to this discussion? Well, my refusal to accept a deficient reading comprehension drove me to work on correcting it. This was my way of balancing that equation (no pun intended). And let me say, after putting ten solid years into this effort, I feel a million times more balanced—as evidenced by this book. Had I attempted this ten years ago, expressing my thoughts in writing would have been difficult, if not impossible.

In these pages is where my newfound balance gets to shine—very cathartic!

CHAPTER 9

Discipline

Desire, determination, dedication, discipline.

In high school I was in three sports: football, track and field, and wrestling. Sports teach us a lot of skills we can apply to our regular lives. Wrestling especially taught me the four Ds: desire, determination, dedication, and discipline.

DESIRE

Desire always struck me as pretty straightforward. We all want things. People in hell want ice water. My daughter wants cake and ice cream for dinner. People at the bottom of a mountain want to be at the top of the mountain. And a lot of us want more money. But no matter what you desire, you first have to decide what you're willing to do to achieve it. This determines whether your desire amounts to anything at all. After all, if you're never going to be willing to do what's required to get it, then you might as well forget it.

DETERMINATION

If desire is the first step, then determination is the second. Once you recognize that you desire something and are willing to put the necessary effort into acquiring it, determination sets you in motion. However, it doesn't necessarily mean that you'll reach your goal.

Say I'm in bed watching TV and want to change the channel, but the remote is missing. I grow determined to get out of bed and change the channel, but instead I decide that what's on is good enough, or perhaps I fall asleep. What if I do get out of bed and walk toward the TV, full of determination, but trip and sprain my ankle?

Determination can wane, and it's no guarantee for success. It moves the ball forward a bit more than desire, but I can still be determined to do something that never quite gets done.

DEDICATION

Dedication is the first real commitment step in the four Ds. But, much like determination, dedication can be fleeting and is not impervious to obstacles. So let's just say that dedication only raises the bar a little. But it's certainly not meaningless. When we dedicate ourselves to something, we link ourselves to it. Through our dedication, we have committed to achieving our goals, and thus can't easily turn away from them. But our weak natures can still muck things up.

DISCIPLINE

Discipline is the final step—and it's the real deal. That's when you stand up as a warrior and hold your ground, come what may. From the big obstacles to the small, from the difficult to the impossible, discipline will push you to overcome. A healthy dose of discipline can go a long way toward success.

It's a powerful word tied to some other heavyweights, like patience, focus, perseverance, stamina, and toughness.

When put in the perspective of, or in conjunction with, balance, discipline takes on even more shape. The two concepts are interconnected; it's impossible to have one without the other. The combination can break down any barrier. And when we realize that our biggest barrier is ourselves, we discover the real power of the combination.

Put these two juggernauts in your tool belt and keep working on building up your proficiency in using them.

CHAPTER 10

Choice

It all comes down to who you serve.

If balance and discipline are perfect bedfellows, then sound choices make that bed even better. Choice—as I perceive it is more than just an action. The world seems to me to revolve around choice. So, to me, it is the most critical element to success.

TIMING AND CHOICES

I've already pointed out the complexities of time against the backdrop of this analysis. However, there is still the business of the title to discuss more explicitly: *Knowledge for the Next Time.*

Let's go back to our three-dimensional selves standing in the living room. Remember the two scenarios: (1) a bag of tax-free money comes crashing through the roof; (2) we're swept away by voodoo pestilence. Same place, two different times. What does choice have to do with those two scenarios?

Well, in the first scenario, maybe you live next to Pablo Escobar. And from your experience, if and when a bag of money falls at your feet, you're better off throwing it back wherever it came from. You've learned a lesson from the past that you can use today to show good judgment in your decisions.

For the second scenario, let's consider it more as a metaphor. Perhaps you're not literally being dragged to hell but instead feel like you are. You might really just be standing in your living room feeling guilty about something you were unable to accomplish. Here, the lesson from your past experiences might be as simple as realizing you did your best. Your choice is to relax; the world's not really ending.

PART IV

Timing is Key

CHAPTER 11

Knowledge for the Next Time

How can I do better? Now you can see that it's not a complicated issue. The layers and nuances it's wrapped up in may be tough to unravel, but the conclusion is pretty straightforward: Learn from your experiences and do better next time. We have enough opportunities. We make repeat decisions all the time, sometimes in the same day.

THE DELTA

A mistake we often make is trying to be something we're not—or at least not yet. Time is the fourth dimension. Slam-dunk champion NBA player might be your destiny, but maybe you're not there just yet. You have to learn how to jump. You need a basketball. You need to grow a few more feet. The point here is we often mistake what we want to be for what we can be right now, and that creates an imbalance—a Delta (δ).

Delta is a letter, Δ or δ, in the Greek alphabet. It's also used as a mathematical symbol. The primary vehicle of calculus and other higher mathematics is a function. That function's "input value" is its argument, usually a point (P) expressible on a graph. The difference between two points is known as their Delta (ΔP), as is the difference in their function result.

You may be saying, "What the front door does this have to do with my self-development? I hate math. Now my head hurts." Understood. Simply put, the Delta is the difference between two points, and for our purposes the two points are Point A, where you believe you are as a person, and Point B, where you really are as a person.

Now, finding your Delta is a very subjective analysis, but there's a simple way to make it more objective. Just honestly answer the following questions: Where do you want to be as an individual? Where do you feel you are today?

If we are honest with ourselves with these most critical questions, then we can measure our progress more objectively. And the distance between where we would say we are at present and where we really are is the Delta. Huge imbalances in our perception of ourselves detract from our ability to be successful in achieving our goals in life. This very real dynamic is often misunderstood or glossed over, but is evident in the simplest of our actions, or inactions.

So for example, if you told your spouse you were going to get the mail by close-of-business on Monday, it's now Friday, and you still haven't done it, it's kind of hard to say you're on top of retrieving the mail. Your Delta is pretty high.

There are infinite examples some that are serious, life-changing issues. For example, the parent who says they never realized they were not emotionally there for their child, until something terrible happened.

Awareness of your truer nature is hard enough, but often it's just a start. With 360 degrees of you to comprehend, self-development takes its own time. Closing the Delta gap is a helpful step, but then comes the work of tweaks and balances.

CONCLUSION

So what have I learned? Always do my best! That's it really. That's all I can do. It seems simple, and it is. And, of course, it's the most oppressive, painful, stressful, taxing, troublesome, complex, complicated, intricate, involved, and problematic objective to achieve.

The obvious takeaway from my lesson is easy to digest: "I can't do better than my best!" On the flipside, however, we might have no idea what our best is. There is often a gap between where we think we are to where we actually are, between how we perceive ourselves and how we actually are (the Delta).

The Delta highlights a difference, and that difference is where we need to make changes. This difference can be small or vast. For example, the level of patience you may think you have may in fact be very different from the level other people perceive you to have. "What do they know?" you ask. Well, you might have a point. However, often we don't even measure up to our own standards.

When I set a goal for myself and don't accomplish it, that shortcoming rests with me—especially when the failure is repeated over time. Think of the eleventy million diets you've started, and your complete failure to lose weight. Six months after you declare you'll clean up the garage, it still looks like the set of *Sanford and Son*. We declare an eight, and we consistently only reach a two. That is the Delta.

We are not perfect beings. So this difference, the Delta, is inherent in our makeup; it's in our DNA. So then what's the problem with it? The problem comes when we don't realize we have a Delta gap in a particular area. Harold has not handled his halitosis very well and insists on only using H-words. He also laughs a lot. "Ha ha ha ha!" Ike Jackson Brown, a local boxer, hasn't come to terms with his aggression out of the ring and is on his third relationship in seven months. Jane often makes insensitive comments to her friends and is oblivious that it bothers them. This causes stress for her friends because it's a problem that has persisted for years.

The next step after you gauge your Delta is to understand your practical potential—that is, how successful your best efforts can be. For example, if you're four feet tall, you might have to put an NBA career in perspective. It's not impossible. But realize that if you do make it to the NBA, you might not be the number one slam-dunker in the game.

It's all about reason over resignation.

Doing your best results in efficiently and effectively succeeding in your life experiences. *Knowledge for the Next Time* is about learning from the past so you can do your best next time and then doing your best throughout your future experiences so that you can be even better after that.

This analysis is predicated on the idea that self-reflection allows your best to keep getting better. Nurturing your personality and feeding the roots of success will allow you to achieve more. Your best self is ever-changing and always growing.

But your best is also as solidly as you can ever attempt to accomplish something. So once you feel you have given a task your best effort, you can rest easy (in the moment). The challenge is figuring out what your best is, what your potential is, and using your experiences to push those limits. But if I can do it, so can you.

Good luck!

POEM

"POW"

==Prisoner of War==

Locked in thought long enough to miss more than
my exit on the freeway. Or the point you were
trying to get across. Too many distractions.

Health ain't healthy. Physical, mental, spiritual. I got
bigger fish to fry. These shackles are all I think about.

Years of my life consumed with grief. It all boiled down to one
thought. Get out. By any means necessary. I went internal.

==A. B. L. Ackman Unchained==

Fewer distractions. Disappointment has been redefined.
Frustrations are duly noted. And then the business of moving

forward is the only real business contemplated and discussed. A conversation of one. Where do we put this? How do we overcome?

SMH. Sons of bitches! You just won't lay down. Have it your way. I'm coming regardless. With my Lord sword gleaming. Light in the darkness. And I will put you down. Hell, I'll put myself down. I'm *always* with me. I can do ten times more damage than you.

I don't need my big stick for this leg. I just got my slingshot. I wish a giant would. Something to lose is not enough anymore. I want it all. Balance, discipline, wisdom, a little clarity, lots of patience. Most of the payment has been made. Just a little more blood. It never ends. But when you turn the corner, everything changes. Happiness.

==New Life==

My lungs filled the air. Is this the afterlife?
Time between blinking. It feels like weeks …
maybe months. I'm focused, man!

Divine vantage point. A reward for persistent patience. All kings are tested. The crucible scorches, but it doesn't burn. It sharpens.

True love. Success. The gates are wide open now. You just take what you want. Rather, what you need. Amazing!

AFTERWORD 2.0

Knowledge for the Next Time has now become a volume of books that are intended to cover a life journey through knowledge, wisdom and understanding, as it applied to success.

> *"Knowledge is the self that has command of an experience. Wisdom is the self that has learned to be shrewd with one's knowledge. Understanding is selfless."*
>
> *- K. Prince*

The topic of human dynamics, or human behavior, as I perceive it, has fascinated me for many years. How might we characterize ourselves and the world around us. More specifically, what makes us tick and what motivates us to keep going. This book flowed from that intrinsic passion, reigniting that spark—the love of the story.

Working on this project has opened up my mind to even more questions, to a broader set of issues related to how people process information. I called this "Afterword 2.0" because this section is a bit more than just an afterword, describing the origin of the book. The real flavor—from the "bone marrow" of the story—came once I put pen to paper. All that to say, it is hard to just talk about what prompted me to write the book, without cooing at what the book has birthed since I began writing it; for example, The Delta and The Aechen Project.

The Delta, which started as a brief discussion in the book highlighting how imbalances in our perception of our self can take away from our walk to wealth, has evolved into its own project. Who are we really, and where do we want to go?

The Aechen Project, is a true gem that will have you feeling like you could really be a superhero. If you enjoyed or felt enriched by any of the topics in this book you must read the synopsis of The Aechen Project in the "*Coming Soon*" section at the very end of the book. I will say, though, that the "improvement function" is a real concept that I instituted back when I was in law school (save for the MRI brain scan), so that might qualify The Aechen Project as properly designated as - based on a true story.

Thank you!

READER'S GUIDE

The feedback I received at the manuscript stage of this book consisted mostly of others' personal experiences and how they related to mine described here. This feedback underscored the universality of many of our experiences as people.

This is a book about using your experiences to do better, but we can also learn from each other. Sharing our stories of how we've dealt with our personal struggles is a powerful tool. Consider discussing the analysis in this book in a group setting, where you can have a chance to see issues from a plurality of different perspectives (See questions below).

My mom is part of a book club. I will call them "The GirlZ" because I think there is only one dude in the group. Shout to mom and her group. When you guys read this just know that I am blessed by your support. Thanks in advance to other book clubs that might read and discuss other projects of mine. Writing is a wonderfully invigorating experience.

Love you!

Here are a few questions to help facilitate group discussion (or personal reflection) on some of the topics touched on in the book.

Before you start, rate your **Delta**. That is, how would you characterize the difference between where you think you are (by your own standard) to where you actually are (being perfectly honest with yourself)? Pick a number from the scale below that you think most closely applies to you?

1-No difference

2-Don't think there's a difference

3-Maybe

4-Probably

5-More than likely

6-Definitely

7-Critical

8-Insane

9-Mental institution

10-Correctional facility (choose one and make note of the number).

Questions

What did Potty Training mean to you? What personal experiences come to mind?

What past experiences did you feel unprepared to face? How do you feel about them today? What present experiences do you feel unprepared to go through? How do you see that developing/changing moving forward?

Do you perceive change from an external perspective, an internal perspective or both and why?

Do you feel you have improved your life (by your own standard)? What do you do that makes you feel like a good person?

What is your main weakness when it comes to food? How do you feel about yummy food commercials that come on late at night?

What are some guilty/sinful pleasures you still dabble in here and there?

What would you consider yourself jaded or apathetic about? How does that affect your relationships?

Do you feel like you hold yourself back? How do you use your trials and tribulations to strengthen yourself? How do you contribute to the problems you face? Do you use past successes to help endure present challenges?

Wealthy vs. Rich: What are the differences? Which do you aspire to?

Faith vs. Hope: What are the differences? Can you have faith but little or no hope?

Who or what do you feel takes the most away from your mental, physical and spiritual vitality?

Wrapping Up

Rate your **Delta** again using the (No difference – Correctional facility) scale above.

Was your score the same as the one you started with? If different, what does that mean to you?

After reading the book, what 'take-a-ways' do you plan to implement in your daily life?

ABOUT THE AUTHOR

Kajli Prince works in the field of intellectual property, with previous professional work in information technology and programming (for stock market trading and back-office processing). Prince has also taught and mentored students of all ages while at University and then later while attending law school. A motivated thinker, conversationalist, and writer, Prince firmly believes that a story is not a story unless one conveys all the details.

An impassioned author, Prince's work focuses on self-development through self-reflection, with autobiographical elements. His broad professional and personal experiences bring vast range and a strong attention to detail to his writing.

Prince lives in Virginia with his wife and daughter.

Coming Soon

Knowledge for the Next Time (Vol. 2)

Knowledge for the Next Time (Vol. 2) examines further how we can all be successful. Volume two continues to look at the difficulties of change, this time from the perspective of trying to be more comfortable with where we are in the process. Patience is arguably counter-intuitive in the face of stress and frustration. How ready are we to trust where awareness and knowledge are taking us?

The Delta

The Delta is an excerpt from the Knowledge for the Next Time volume of books that has evolved into a much more in-depth look at the often glaring imbalance(s) in our perception of our self. It is an examination stretching from who we have been and feel we are today, to our present person and who we would like to be in the future. Who and what we care about the most say the most about our character. What do you see when you close your eyes?

The Aechen Project

The Aechen Project is an original screenplay about a group of disenfranchised inner city youth who go from obscurity to being the face of a nation. Based on the simple notion of—*rewarding improvement*, this group demonstrates that the human being will always be the most complex and technologically advanced functioning "machine" in existence.

The story delves into the emerging field of educational neuroscience. Dr. Michael Larkin has developed an "improvement function"—$f(\mathfrak{p})$. The function is comprised of variables based on applied science—e.g. neural mapping measurements acquired using MRI technology, as well as variables derived from standardized and non-standardized psychometric tests, and a *key* variable known as "The Delta." But this national security level project has been exposed and the powers that be realize they face extinction given the ability Larkin's *improvement function* has to unleash the full potential of man's most primal source of existence—the brain.

The Aechen Project is a story about humanity's infinite potential, and our faith in the hope that our commitment to one another still makes a difference.

Printed in the United States
By Bookmasters